Supplement to *British Book News*: No. 30

SAMUEL BUTLER

By G. D. H. COLE

PUBLISHED FOR
THE BRITISH COUNCIL
and the NATIONAL BOOK LEAGUE
by LONGMANS, GREEN & CO.
LONDON. NEW YORK. TORONTO.

Revised Price
2s. 6d. net

Professor Cole, who was born in 1889, has had a most distinguished academic career, notably in the study and exposition of Social and Political Theory. But his literary interests are wide: they include William Cobbett, William Morris, and Samuel Butler, all of whom concerned themselves, at least to some degree, with the structure and imperfections of the society of their time. Moreover, he and his wife, Margaret Cole, who is also an expert in social and economic problems, have over thirty years collaborated in a series of detective stories which have won the appreciation of followers of this exacting craft.

In this essay Professor Cole follows up an assessment, published in 1947, of *Samuel Butler and* 'THE WAY OF ALL FLESH', giving a concise survey of Butler's whole output, and of his effect on his own and later generations.

Samuel Butler died just fifty years ago, and there is every sign that he will continue to inspire lively critical comment. Professor Cole's essay is particularly apposite, coming at such a time and from such an authoritative source.

Bibliographical Series
of Supplements to ' British Book News '

*

GENERAL EDITOR
T. O. Beachcroft

SAMUEL BUTLER

from a painting of 1896 by his friend CHARLES GOGIN
in the National Portrait Gallery.

SAMUEL BUTLER

By G. D. H. COLE

PUBLISHED FOR
THE BRITISH COUNCIL
and the NATIONAL BOOK LEAGUE
BY LONGMANS, GREEN & CO., LONDON, NEW YORK, TORONTO

LONGMANS, GREEN & CO. LTD.
6 & 7 Clifford Street, London, W.1
Also at Melbourne and Cape Town

LONGMANS, GREEN & CO. INC.
55 Fifth Avenue, New York, 3

LONGMANS, GREEN & CO.
215 Victoria Street, Toronto, 1

ORIENT LONGMANS LTD.
Bombay, Calcutta, Madras

First published in 1952

Printed in Great Britain by Benham and Company Limited
Colchester

CONTENTS

I	THE MAN	*page* 7
II	HIS BOOKS	22
III	*EREWHON*—AND A SUMMING-UP	37
	A SELECT BIBLIOGRAPHY	45

⁋ SAMUEL BUTLER was born on 4 December 1835 at Langar, near Bingham, Nottinghamshire. He died in London on 18 June 1902.

SAMUEL BUTLER

I

THE MAN

SAMUEL BUTLER, sometimes called '*Erewhon*' Butler to distinguish him from his seventeenth-century namesake, the author of *Hudibras*, was born in 1835 and died in 1902. His best-known book in his own day was *Erewhon*, that amusing satire on the conventions and standards of his age ; but of late he has been better known as the author of *The Way of All Flesh*, his only true novel, which was composed over many years, but published only after his death. His writings make up a curious collection. There are the stories—*The Way of All Flesh*, *Erewhon* and its sequel *Erewhon Revisited*, and the satirical memoir of an imaginary John Pickard Owen which forms the opening part of his essay in the higher criticism, *The Fair Haven*. Then there are four books, beginning with *Life and Habit*, in which he sets forth his own theory of creative evolution and attacks the Darwinians. These books have never been widely read; but the popularization of some of their ideas by Bernard Shaw has given Butler's theory a currency much wider than it got in his lifetime. Next come two books about Italy and his wanderings there—*Alps and Sanctuaries* and *Ex Voto*—both concerned with the people and, most of all, with the arts in their setting of land and people. Akin to these, because it took Butler to Sicily and has a similar setting, is that queer book, *The Authoress of the Odyssey*, in which he tried to prove that that poem was composed by a Sicilian woman and that the geography of Odysseus' wanderings is that of Sicily and the neighbouring lands. Nor is this the only oddity—another is his edition and rearrangement of Shakespeare's *Sonnets*, in which he attempted to reconstruct the story lying behind them, in such a way as to infuriate Shakespearian scholars as much as he had already enraged in turn the biblical critics, the Darwinians, and the classical experts. Samuel Butler loved to invert an accepted theory or belief as much as he enjoyed turning a familiar proverb upside down to make a paradox which was also usually a statement at least of a half-truth.

The list of Butler's miscellaneous writings is not yet nearly exhausted. His first book, edited by his father to such an extent that he ever after refused to recognize any merit in it, was a straightforward account of his experiences as an up-country sheep-farmer in New Zealand, whither he had gone after he had fled in dismay from his expected destiny as a clergyman. He translated both the *Iliad* and the *Odyssey* into colloquial prose, which failed to catch the taste of his generation but is much more in harmony with later ideas of the translator's art. He wrote a full-length biography of his grandfather, the Samuel Butler who was in succession headmaster of Shrewsbury and a zealous bishop—conscious amends for the misunderstanding of a man he had disliked by instinct because of his feeling that headmasters and bishops were *ex hypothesi* dislikeable, but had taken a fancy to, when, on inheriting his papers, he discovered what sort of man he had really been. Over and above all this, Butler published a number of essays and pamphlets; joined with his close friend, Henry Festing Jones, in composing a considerable number of musical pieces in a style reminiscent of Handel—for whom he had an enthusiasm accorded to no other musician and to no other man save Shakespeare; wrote several really remarkable sonnets and at least one unforgettable other composition in verse (*A Psalm of Montreal*); painted a number of pictures by no means without merit; and, last but not least, left behind, in his *Note-books*, a series of pungent and often both penetrating and amusing comments on life, art, and letters which now take rank, with *The Way of All Flesh*, as the most remarkable of all his writings.

This is not, for a professional author and creative artist, at all a long, though it is an unusually varied, list. But, in effect, Butler never really was a professional—if he had been, he would certainly have starved. His books, save *Erewhon*, never sold largely ; his painting, after a hopeful start, petered out ; his music had practically no public at all. He never lived by his creative work, and never made any appreciable amount of money after he ceased to be a sheep-farmer. He was never a wealthy man ; but he was never without private means, though till his father died he was often straitened for money and at one point came near ruin through unfortunate speculations into which he was tempted by his friend Hoare, the banker. For many years he went short because of the quixotry with which he supported an unworthy friend, Charles Pauli, who battened meanly upon him ; but he was never in real straits. He wrote what he felt like writing without making any concession to the public and for the most part paid out of his own pocket the cost of producing his books. Again and again he is found, in the *Note-books*, commenting ruefully on his financial ill-success, and more than half resenting it as the fault of critics and pundits who refused to do him justice. But, though his isolation hurt his pride, nothing would have induced him to alter his behaviour in the smallest degree in order to escape from it. He liked, as well as resented, being a lone wolf.

In a way, this was strange in him ; for in a good many respects he was a very conventional person. The kind of man he most admired was one who, unburdened with much philosophy, but armed with unselfconscious self-confidence and good health and good manners, went through life carrying things before him with a high but not a heavy hand, secure in the possession of an assured bank balance and an inheritance of gentlemanly blood. He had a great belief in the virtues of gentility and of ' well-to-do-ness ' : his unorthodoxy in other respects left untouched his essential upper-middle-classness in estimating matters of practical conduct. His devastating criticism of Victorian family life did not prevent him from having a strong sense of family unity. His attacks on the Victorian public school did not stop him from attending devoutly the ' old boy ' reunions of his own school—Shrewsbury. Once bit by financial speculation, he fell back on an almost reverent worship of gilt-edged securities. This last devotion he even expressed in verse and set to music.

> How blest the prudent man, the maiden pure,
> Whose income is both ample and secure,
> Arising from Consolidated Three
> Per cent Annuities, paid quarterly.

And, what is more, he meant all this. Towneley, in *The Way of All Flesh*, and George, in *Erewhon Revisited*, are Butler's two presentations of the ideal man; for himself and for others who lacked the gifts he most admired, his prescription of the next best was a quiet, outwardly respectable, life on a secure income from prudently invested capital. He made no pretence of liking the poor, unless, like Italian peasants, they could be poor gracefully. He regarded a social conscience, which was coming into fashion in his middle age, as a tiresome and unnecessary burden: he insisted again and again on men's *duty* to make themselves happy and comfortable as far as they could, because he found happy and comfortable persons by far the most pleasant to consort with.

I have written 'outwardly respectable', because that is what Butler would have wished me to write. The sin he chiefly reprobated was being found out: he said many times that what mattered to a man was his reputation. He had no qualms about maintaining a lady—'Madame'—to whom he resorted regularly for many years of his bachelor existence; and one is left in some doubt—real doubt—about his doings in the course of his Italian jaunts, and even about the nature of his relations with Pauli during the earlier phases of their intercourse. It may be that, apart from 'Madame', his conduct was at all times as exemplary as he wished it to appear; whether or no, it is simply taking him at his word to assert that he estimated the appearance of respectability well above the reality.

Of one thing there is no doubt : Butler had a horror of getting married. Whether he was at any time in danger of it remains an open question : in certain of his moods he certainly thought he was. This brings us to a consideration of the one great friendship of his life that was not with a man—the intimate connexion with Miss Savage that was ended only by her death. He was thirty-one when they met as art students attending the same school. Butler had then published nothing except his book on his New Zealand experiences, a pamphlet on the evidence for the Resurrection—to be expanded later into *The Fair Haven*—and a few articles. He was still trying to find himself as a painter, and had no intention of taking seriously to authorship. He and Miss Savage began writing to each other regularly as well as meeting, and the friendship soon developed into a close intellectual intimacy. The earlier letters are lost : the extant correspondence between them begins in 1871, and was edited by Butler himself after her death, but not published in full till 1935, though much of it had appeared in 1920 in Henry Festing Jones's *Memoir*. Miss Savage's letters are both astonishingly witty and living, and supremely helpful to Butler as a writer. Without her, it is certain that *The Way of All Flesh* would never have been written, and doubtful whether Butler would ever have settled down to serious writing. Whether she had any large share in the making of *Erewhon* does not appear—he began writing it about two years after their meeting. That in the shaping of *The Way of All Flesh* her share was great indeed the letters leave in no doubt : so keen was Butler's own sense of this that when she died, in 1885, he put the book away, only half re-written with her aid, and never touched it again. Nor can it be disputed that what he had revised was immensely better than the rest.

The nature of the relations between these two as novelist and literary midwife are clear enough, and immensely interesting. It is much less clear what else was between them. Butler has left on record some very strange comments on

Miss Savage in both prose and verse, including at one point —in an account written long after her death—the astonishing remark that she 'bored' him, and at a number the assertion that she wanted him to marry her. He expressed remorse again and again, when she was dead, because of his conduct towards her and of his inability to give her what he thought she wanted. He described, in verse, her lack of physical attraction

> For she was plain and lame and fat and short,
>   Forty and over-kind. Hence it befell
> That though I loved her in a certain sort,
>   Yet did I love too wisely, but not well.

He wrote—not for publication in his lifetime, but preserved among his papers—most ungenerously, as well as remorsefully about her. He was clearly afraid of her, at the same time as he was deeply enjoying her friendship. But whether he was right about what she wanted, or at any rate allowed herself to want, who can say ? It seems much more likely that Miss Savage, knowing her own disabilities—among them, a form of hip-disease—was content with the mutual gift of friendship, and, consciously at all events, asked for no more. The rest can easily have been due to Butler's deep-rooted fear of being caught—a fear which haunted him most of his life. He was afraid of being caught by his father, of being caught by the Church, for which he was originally destined, of being caught by sheep-farming, so that he could not escape, of being caught by a wife, whether Miss Savage or another. He was for ever wriggling out of the grasp of something, or of somebody ; and he always wanted very much to make his escape without loss of his own or other people's respect. Unconventional though he was in many of his ideas, he was set on being, or at least on appearing, conventional in his behaviour. Butler had a timid man's respect for the society he satirized : Miss Savage, too, was conventional in behaviour, but she had much less respect than he had for the world around her. Her letters show her continually egging him on : his are sometimes those of a rather frightened man, but suggest that he was afraid much more, while she lived, of being led too far intellectually than of being made love to, even in the most indirect way.

However all this may really have been, there is no doubt either about the quality of Miss Savage's letter-writing or about the influence she had on Butler as an imaginative artist. Nor is there any doubt that, on Butler's side, the friendship with her was purely intellectual, and had no physical element. Almost at the same time as he began writing *The Way of All Flesh* he took up with Lucie Dumas ('Madame'), who for the next twenty years supplied what he required, not only as a 'he-man' but also in restful, un-intellectual companionship. Miss Savage's place, after her death, was increasingly filled by Henry Festing Jones, who had the advantage over her of not being a woman, so that they could go about freely together and no fears of capture were aroused in Butler's mind. Jones shared with Butler, as Miss Savage had done, the relish for turning proverbs and ideas upside down or inside out ; but there the resemblance ended. As a writer, Butler got nothing out of Jones except appreciation. He enjoyed being and doing things with Jones ; and their friendship helped to turn his attention towards musical composition and towards writing about art and about Italy. But there was in Jones no such original force as there had been in Miss Savage.

Of Butler's other friendships only two seem to have touched him deeply, and both were with men. Of his relations with Charles Paine Pauli he has left a circumstantial, but nevertheless rather bewildering, account. Butler first met Pauli in New Zealand, ill and penniless, brought him back to England and, with what seems astonishing generosity, agreed to contribute heavily to his support until he could make enough money as a barrister to stand on his own feet. This support was continued for many years, even when Butler himself was in serious financial difficulties. It was continued in face of Pauli's repeated failures to give any account of his financial circumstances, and despite the evident disappearance on Pauli's part of any affection or desire for Butler's intimacy. Only when Pauli died did Butler find out that he had been for many years making quite a good income and was even in possession of a substantial amount of capital—how acquired was never explained, though Butler, in his account of the affair, offers a plausible guess. On Butler's side, there was clearly something that made him feel bound to Pauli long after he knew that the man had ceased to care for him and at least half knew that he was being deceived. For years Pauli came to lunch with Butler once a week : they must have been uncomfortable meetings, for Butler was well aware that often Pauli did not want to come and took no pleasure in his society. Pauli never told Butler where he was living, never invited him back, never told him about his friends or doings, never revealed that he was getting help from other sources—among them Swinburne. At one time, Butler must have loved Pauli deeply ; and nothing that Pauli did or failed to do later could wipe away his sense of being bound to him—nothing, that is, till Pauli died and the full story of his deceptions came out. The affair lasted for a third of a century, and cost Butler dear in lacerated feelings as well as in hard cash.

The other friendship, begun three years before Pauli's death in 1897, was with a young Swiss, Hans Faesch, to whom Butler addressed a moving poem on his departure for the Far East. That was a friendship shared with Jones ; we know little of it except that it mattered to Butler a great deal. There were other friendships—with Gogin the painter[1] and, in his later years, with friends made in Italy and Sicily in the course of his journeyings—but these four—with Pauli, with Miss Savage, with Festing Jones, and with Hans Faesch—clearly counted for most in his life.

As for his enmities, only one went really deep. His

[1] Charles Gogin exhibited at the Royal Academy between 1874 and 1894. His portrait of Butler was a late work (see Frontispiece).

literary quarrels, his *fracas* with Darwin, his bickerings with all the pundits it was ever his fortune to encounter, were minor matters in comparison with his feelings of enmity towards his father. This, however, was not unmixed : there was something in him that forbade him quite to break away from his family, or to renounce a sense of being bound to Canon Butler despite his animosity and the bruised sense of grievance that never left him to the end of his life. How far this grievance was real or imaginary must always remain a moot point. Butler's account of his father's character is not easily squared with what we know from other sources ; yet the conflicting versions are not wholly irreconcilable. On the son's showing, his father always disliked him and tried instinctively to thwart him at every important point in his career ; but Butler would not have disputed a statement that Canon Butler disapproved of his son and attempted to control his actions for his good. He would only have commented that the disapproval was a rationalization of the dislike, and the attempted control the outcome of an unquestioning self-righteousness. The Canon's act in editing and publishing *A First Year in Canterbury Settlement*, based on his son's graphic letters home, was not that of a man who was set on putting the son down, or without appreciation of his qualities. Yet it became, for the son, a leading count in the indictment. Butler came to *loathe* the book because of his father's part in it, and to be utterly blind to its merits. He could see only what Canon Butler had cut out—cuts which must have been vastly aggravating, but are evidence of no more than an antipathy to dangerous thoughts. The Canon was beyond question a most respectable clergyman, of highly conventional mind, with a terror of unorthodox or subversive opinions. He could not be expected to like, or not strongly to disapprove of, his son's attitude to life, or not to be shocked when his son first rejected the clerical career for which he had been brought up, and then proceeded from rejection to religious doubt, and presently to positive infidelity. Apart from this, there are passages in *The Way of All Flesh* which suggest that Canon Butler may have had other, more narrowly moral, grounds for disapproval of his son's conduct ; and the packing off of the offender to the Colonies fits in neatly to make a familiar Victorian pattern. It must not be forgotten, either, that the son went off quite handsomely endowed, and was able to buy a profitable sheep-run and, after only a few years, to return with enough money of his own not only to live the life he planned, irrespective of his father's wishes, but also to maintain Charles Pauli in face of his father's protest. Butler's intention then was to become a painter—for which he had some talent, but not enough. Though in due course he exhibited at the Royal Academy, his best picture was painted in 1864, the first year of his apprenticeship ; and it is significant that its subject was ' Family Prayers ', and its scene laid in the paternal rectory. Canon Butler did not wish his son to become an artist, of any sort, and must have disliked this particular picture quite strongly, if he ever saw it. The son put all this down to his father's dislike of him and desire to thwart him and to control his life. The father, no doubt, felt, over and above a belief that the arts were not quite respectable, a special mistrust of putting such dangerous weapons as financial independence into the hands of the prodigal son. For many years afterwards the two continued to dispute about money—the more when Butler, involved in his friend Hoare's unsuccessful speculations, had got into financial trouble, and wanted his father, by joining with him in cutting off an entail, to come to his rescue. The Canon had, no doubt, a feeling of ' I told you so ', as well as a fear of throwing good money after bad : the son regarded his father's attitude as yet another example of the will to keep him in subjection. So it went on ; but Canon Butler in the end did cut the entail of his own accord, and did leave his money to his son when he died.

There can, I think, be no question that Butler did some injustice to his father, both in the portrait of Theobald Pontifex in *The Way of All Flesh* and in his private jottings on the subject of their relations. They were two men who were bound to clash continually, and to fail to come to any understanding. The Canon can have been in no doubt concerning his son's thoughts about him; and these were not of a sort to make it easy for him to behave well. If Charlotte Yonge, that rival portrait-painter of the Victorian family group, had written her story of the Pontifex family we should have seen the other side, and very interesting the contrast would have been.

Towards his mother Butler never showed animosity; but both in *The Fair Haven*, which was published in his lifetime, and in *The Way of All Flesh*, which was not, he ridiculed her day-dreaming and poked cruel fun at her ideas of the duty of a wife and mother. In *The Way* he ran his two sisters, one of whom only he really disliked, into a most unpleasing composite portrait. The one nice member of the Pontifex family, Alethea, was drawn not from a Butler but from Miss Savage. Ernest Pontifex, for whom Butler was himself the model, hardly qualifies for the adjective. The only Butler of whom he ever wrote in high laudation was his grandfather, the headmaster-bishop; and that was by way of amends, in the mellower afternoon of life, long after his father's death and after he had put *The Way of All Flesh* away in a drawer and turned to the joys of combat with other antagonists.

I have said that Butler had a horror of getting married. Even more fundamentally, he had a horror of family life. The family household, in the form in which he had experienced it and had learnt to imagine it, filled him with sentiments of repulsion and desire to escape. There is a passage in the *Note-books* in which, using the Erewhonian conception of the importunity of the 'unborn' to induce someone to bring them into the world, Butler speculates about his relations with a supposititious son.

> I have often told my son that he must begin by finding me a wife to become his mother who shall satisfy both himself and me. But this is only one of the many rocks on which we have

hitherto split. We should never have got on together. I should have had to cut him off with a shilling either for laughing at Homer, or for refusing to laugh at him, or both, or neither, but still cut him off. So I settled the matter long ago by turning a deaf ear to his importunities and sticking to it that I would not get him at all. Yet his thin ghost visits me at times, and though he knows that it is no use pestering me further, he looks at me so wistfully and reproachfully that I am half-inclined to turn tail, take my chance about his mother and ask him to let me get him after all. But I should show a clean pair of heels if he said ' Yes '.

Besides, he would probably be a girl.

Butler had not enjoyed being a son, and he did not like the idea of being a father. Nor had he liked the relations between his parents, and he had no taste for being a husband. What he did like was being let alone to go his own way ; and the entire system of the family seemed to him to deny this boon. This too is from the *Note-books*. ' I could stand my relations well enough if they would only let me alone. It is my relations with my relations that I sometimes find embarrassing.' So is this, about Melchisedec. ' He was a really happy man. He was without father, without mother, and without descent. He was an incarnate bachelor. He was a born orphan.'

The family, of which Butler felt so deep a dislike, had reached its apotheosis in the novel-writing of the Victorian era. The immense family chronicles of Charlotte Yonge— a very much better novelist than could be recognized until the age of revolt against the Victorian family conventions was over—present this pattern of living at its most complete development. Charlotte Yonge's characters are highly individual ; but they are shown to the reader as working parts of a larger whole—the household family with its endless ramifications and interconnexions with in-laws and friends who have become adopted members of the family group. The Charlotte Yonge household is never isolated : its life branches out in many directions and its contacts keep it always in active touch with a wider environment. It is limited, no doubt, by an acute sense of class-distinctions—above all, because of the sharp distinction drawn between those who are 'gentlemen' and 'ladies' and those who, however worthy or wealthy, are not. But its circle is wide enough to include a large diversity of creatures, including 'the poor', who are allowed to have characters of their own, provided they demean themselves suitably towards their 'betters'. By contrast with this, the family as seen by Butler is almost an isolated group of parents and children, shut up together in a box and forced to exercise on one another their talents for disagreeable behaviour. Charlotte Yonge's characters are, of course, sometimes disagreeable one to another ; but for the most part they are too busy to have time to be really unpleasant. Butler's, on the other hand, find infinite leisure for treading on one another's corns. The Pontifex household, as Butler describes it, lives almost in a Hobbesian 'state of nature', with parents warring against children, and child against child. The family, which for Charlotte Yonge is a natural centre of mutual affection and goodwill, is for Butler no less natural, but of its very nature a jungle of mutual antagonisms and dislikes.

No doubt, this difference is partly the result of different personal experience. Charlotte Yonge is most at home with big families : the Butlerian family is much less philoprogenitive. Charlotte Yonge's families are commonly rather short of money : Butler's Pontifixes have rather more than they well know how to spend. Property, will-making, and financial prudence have their part in Charlotte Yonge's plots ; but they are hardly ever dominant themes, as they are apt to be in the lesser stories of Anthony Trollope and of many other Victorian writers. In this respect Butler resembles Trollope, but with an exaggerated insistence on the will-shaking father who uses the money-power to dominate the lives of his children. Moreover, in Butler's presentation the women get no sort of a chance. The Butlerian family is thoroughly patriarchal, with the mother compensating in day-dreams for her entire subordination to the father in the actual business of life.

This contrast may appear to rest on too narrow a foundation, in that Butler in effect painted the picture only of a single household—or at most of a single family through two successive generations. As a novelist he had little independent power of imagination : for the most part he could only record, satirize and caricature what he had experienced —or thought he had—in his own person.

This personal experience of Butler's was of a peculiar kind of household—that of a well-to-do Victorian cleric in a country parish where there was a lack of congenial neighbours and, for a man neither addicted to good works nor able to make friends outside his class, too little to do. The Butlers (and the Pontifexes) were no doubt an abnormal household ; but Canon Butler's son was conditioned to seeing them as typical ; and, in some respects at least, though not in all, they were.

I am not sure how clearly any portrait of Butler himself has emerged from this account of his attitudes to other people. It should have ; for such attitudes are a great part of a man. But it can hardly have emerged entire ; for Butler was a strongly self-centred person, much preoccupied with making his personal accommodation with life. He combined with his self-centredness an excessive sensitiveness to criticism which rested at bottom on self-mistrust. His aggressiveness in controversy, his readiness to attribute bad motives, his pained surprise when the victims of his pen hit back, all proceeded, I think, from self-doubt. He wanted very much to believe that everything he did was worth while, not merely for his own satisfaction, but in its own independent right ; but quite often he was not sure. He needed applause ; and, except from Miss Savage, Jones, and a few others, he got little of it. He wanted his books to pay, not only because he could have done with the money, but also because he admired success and wanted it to be proved for him that he was not a failure. But, of all his books, only *Erewhon* sold well in his lifetime ; and of *Erewhon* he had no very high opinion. Believing he had written much better and more important things, or at any rate believing this with most of his mind, he was ready to attack his critics as dishonestly crying him down or keeping a conspiracy of silence—the readier because at the back of his mind was a doubt whether he was really achieving anything after all. The achievement about which he was least doubtful was embodied in his four books on Evolution, which had the double distinction in his lifetime of being attacked and unread save by a very few. In this field at any rate he felt sure he was ' on to ' something important ; but, unhappily for him, he spoke a language which his generation was totally unable to understand. His contemporaries thought —indeed he himself thought—that he was writing about biology from a standpoint essentially different from Darwin's, when in reality what he had to say was for the most part not biology at all, but social psychology, at a time when, in Great Britain, such a subject hardly existed. A lot of biology got tangled up in his argument ; but essentially what he was writing about was the function and modification of habit in societies, human and animal, and the function of memory, conscious and unconscious, in the social inheritance of the race. For this to be understood, he had to wait both for an interpreter and for a generation attuned to listen. Bernard Shaw took on the interpreter's function ; and in the mental atmosphere of the twentieth century his ideas have come to be much better understood, though there is much failure to appraise them at their full value even now. To-day, Butler's paradoxes—and he loved a paradox above most things—have ceased to be as startling as they once were. His picture of the Victorian family has become a period piece ; the Darwinism he attacked has ceased to be sacred, or anathema ; realistic discussion of Shakespeare's *Sonnets* is no longer taboo ; the biographers can write about Butler, if not quite freely, much more freely than, even in the guise of fiction, he could ever have written about himself. Butler is now a 'classic', if only a minor one : he has been vindicated, as he hoped but never fully expected to be, by the praise and interest of men living after him. In his own day, however, he was always something of a misfit, and, partly because he was a misfit, particularly in his own family, unsure of himself, and accordingly the more disposed to try to reassure himself by aggression, and to shrink back from its consequences behind a protective colouring of practical respectability and abstinence from disturbing social contacts. Such, I think, was the man : it remains to say something more about his achievements as an artist.

II

HIS BOOKS

Samuel Butler's earliest published writings, apart from a few pieces of undergraduate journalism, were the book, *A First Year in Canterbury Settlement*, which his father edited from the letters and descriptions he sent home from New Zealand, and a number of occasional contributions to the New Zealand *Press*—among them the germ of 'The Book of the Machines' in *Erewhon*. At this stage in his development he had no intention of becoming a regular writer— any more than he was resigned to spending the rest of his life as a sheep-farmer. He had but recently made an almost last-minute escape from becoming a clergyman—a destiny which he seems to have taken for granted at his parents' behest till he woke up suddenly to a sense of the awful irrevocability of it. His drawing back does not appear, even then, to have been mainly—though it was in part— an outcome of religious 'doubt' : indeed, he seems to have taken his religion, as well as much else, for granted very easily right through his time at Cambridge. His initial revolt was much more against being turned into what he called later a 'walking Sunday' and being called on to spend his life in 'good works' and mixing with the 'deserving poor '. A short period in a slum parish convinced him that he did not like the poor ; and he sturdily maintained his antipathy in later life, subject to certain exceptions among the ' undeserving ' who amused him. His ' doubts ' seem to have come mainly after his act of rejection, and to have grown upon him while he was up country in New Zealand, with plenty of time on his hands for solitary meditation as he rode his rounds. They were, superficially, the ' doubts ' of his generation, deriving their content partly from the 'Higher Criticism' of which Strauss had been the pioneer and partly from the heated contemporary discussion aroused by Darwin's *The Origin of Species*, which appeared just as he was settling down in New Zealand. His contributions to the New Zealand *Press* show that he was thinking seriously about Darwinism while he tended his sheep ; and when he got back to England after five years' absence the first thing he published (in 1865) was an anonymous pamphlet entitled *The Evidence for the Resurrection of Jesus Christ as given by the Four Evangelists critically examined*.

Butler's argument in this pamphlet, reproduced later in an expanded form in *The Fair Haven*, was that there existed no good evidence of the Resurrection having ever occurred. Christ, he suggested, had not died upon the Cross : he had been taken down for dead, and his still living body had been removed from the tomb in which it had been laid. Joseph of Arimathea had harboured him and nursed him back to health ; and his appearances to his disciples after the Crucifixion had thus been in no wise out of the order of nature. Having reached this conclusion, Butler remained satisfied with it for the rest of his life and made no further ventures into the field of the ' Higher Criticism '. Instead, he applied much the same approach to showing that the *Odyssey* had been written in Sicily by a young lady, and to piecing together an interpretation of the love-story underlying Shakespeare's *Sonnets*.

The problems raised by Darwin could not be so easily exorcized. When *The Origin of Species* came into Butler's hands very soon after its publication, he became—in his own words—' one of Mr. Darwin's many enthusiastic admirers, and wrote a philosophical dialogue (the most offensive form, except poetry and books of travel into supposed unknown countries, that even literature can assume) upon *The Origin of Species*.' This dialogue appeared in the New Zealand *Press*, and someone sent Darwin a copy: he expressed admiration for it, and recommended publication in England—an odd beginning for the relations between the two. For Butler, after receiving Darwin's book with enthusiasm, grew gradually more and more critical of it, till he came to reject altogether the place given to Natural Selection in the Darwinian theory and to re-assert against it the older theory of Creative Evolution professed by Lamarck and by Charles Darwin's grandfather, Erasmus Darwin. This, however, did not happen at once, or till much thinking had gone into the working out of Butler's own attitude.

Butler, before his half-enforced emigration to New Zealand, had wanted to be a painter, but had been met by his father's uncompromising refusal to allow him a penny towards the cost of apprenticeship to such a career. If he would not be a clergyman, Canon Butler demanded that he should become either a lawyer or a schoolmaster; but he would be neither. He preferred emigration, and, Canterbury Settlement having been chosen for him because of its sound, Church of England principles, the Canon came down not unhandsomely with the capital needed to give him a start. Butler did well with the money; but his heart was not in sheep-farming, and as soon as he felt able to meet the costs of learning to be a painter, he sold out and came back, more determined than ever that painting was to be his life's work.

Between 1865 and 1872 Butler published literally nothing. He was learning to be a painter, and then endeavouring to practise the art he had learnt. In 1869 he first exhibited at the Royal Academy; and he continued to do this until

1876. By the following year, when the Academy rejected his pictures, he had made up his mind that he would never succeed as a painter. He said later that he believed he might have made more of his painting if he had stuck to his own style, instead of allowing himself to be guided by academic conventions; and this is probably correct, for, as we have seen, he painted one of his best pictures right at the beginning of his period of attendance at the schools. He began writing again in 1870, when a friend suggested that he should work up his early New Zealand articles about Darwinism and kindred subjects into a book. This was the origin of *Erewhon*, at which he worked only in the evenings, after the day's work at painting, and with no thought of taking to regular authorship. He began *Erewhon* not long after becoming friendly with Miss Savage; and when it was done with, he began, with her encouragement, the first draft of *The Way of All Flesh*. His next published book, however, was *The Fair Haven*—in its main text a development of his pamphlet about the evidence for the Resurrection, but memorable above all for the most amusing 'spoof' biography with which he introduced it to the world. This purported to be a memoir of the imaginary author of the book, John Pickard Owen, written by his imaginary brother; and it is notable for the picture of the mother of the two Owens, whose day-dreams of her children's future go far beyond the dreamings attributed to Christina Pontifex in *The Way of All Flesh*. The entire memoir is most entertaining—so much so that it is difficult to credit that it was ever taken seriously. Eminent clerics, however, did both accept it at its face value and allow themselves to be taken in by the rest of the book, which consisted of an ironical defence of the miraculous elements in the story of Christ against infidel 'higher critics'—a defence in which every argument was so turned as to render it ridiculous. The book was, of course, published without Butler's name, as the work of the Owens; and when the deceived clerics discovered the hoax they were naturally very cross. Butler, as an author, had scored his first bad conduct mark in the respectable world : he was soon to increase his score, and to stir up more serious animosities. As he wrote later, ' I attacked the foundations of morality in *Erewhon*, and nobody cared two straws. I tore open the wounds of my Redeemer as he hung upon the Cross in *The Fair Haven*, and people rather liked it. But when I attacked Mr. Darwin they were up in arms in a moment.' This was not quite true : *Erewhon* was, no doubt, regarded as a good joke, but *The Fair Haven* did give offence, though not to the same persons as were outraged by Butler's presuming to cross swords with Darwin. Butler disclosed his authorship of *The Fair Haven* in a second edition, published the same year as the first ; but thereafter came a second break in his career as a writer. He produced nothing more until *Life and Habit* appeared, more than four years later.

The break was due partly to the fact that even in 1873 he was still set on painting rather than on writing, but also to the financial troubles which fell on him in 1874, when the companies in which he had invested on his friend, Hoare's, advice collapsed, and he went to Canada in the hope of saving something from the wreck of his fortunes. He was in Canada for a good part of the next two years, for the most part heavily occupied in business. His sojourn there produced one tiny, but most entertaining, piece of writing, *A Psalm of Montreal*, with its now familiar refrain, ' O God ! O Montreal ! ', but nothing else. He came back to England in 1875, having saved a little of his money, but not much, and had then to decide what he meant to do with the rest of his life. He was forty-two, and short of money, though he had comfortable expectations of what he would get, despite their differences, when his father died.

It was at this point, or soon after, that Butler went over definitely to writing, though he was never in fact to write another book that sold nearly as well as *Erewhon*—I mean while he lived. In 1876 he began writing *Life and Habit*, the first of his books on evolutionary theory, and the best. It carried, when it appeared late the following year, the subtitle *An Essay after a Complete View of Evolution*. A second edition appeared within a year. *Evolution Old and New*, a much more direct attack on the Darwinian hypothesis, followed in 1879, and *Unconscious Memory*, containing a further attack, in 1880. The last of this series of books, *Luck or Cunning as the main means of Organic Modification ?* was not published until 1886.

During these years Butler, in addition to working up his contribution to the theory of evolution, returned for a short time to his speculations on theology. In 1879 he published in *The Examiner* two series of articles—*A Clergyman's Doubts*, written under the disguise indicated by the title, and *God the Known and God the Unknown*, which was issued as a book after his death. Thereafter theology ceased to attract him : he had worked it out of his system and reached the comfortable conclusion that it was equally foolish to expend pen and ink on affirming or denying God's existence. As he wrote in one of his note-books, under the heading 'Theist and Atheist', 'The fight between them is as to whether God shall be called God or shall have some other name'. In another place he described 'God' as a convenient label it was too much of a nuisance to do without. At the conventional God of the religious he continued to poke fun to the end of his life ; but he lost his zeal in proselytizing about the matter as soon as, like Ernest Pontifex in *The Way of All Flesh*, he had settled to his own satisfaction that there was nothing in it that need affect either his happiness or his conduct.

With Darwinism it was otherwise. Butler's entire conception of himself and of mankind as seen mainly by looking at himself forbade him to accept Natural Selection from among chance, or at least unexplained, 'variations' as the main force in the development of species. He wanted and could not be satisfied without a theory of evolution that put the stress on the effects of conscious striving. He wanted to believe that the species changed and adapted themselves by trying and learning, and were not merely passive victims of natural selection. Such a theory, however, clearly could not be sustained unless there were some way in which acquired characteristics, and especially learning acquired in one generation, could be transmitted to descendants. Accordingly, Butler went back to the older versions of the evolutionary doctrine, which accepted this principle of positive adaptation and transmission, and set out to explain how the process worked. This led him to the emphasis which he laid on the formation of habits as a means of establishing direct, unconscious responses to familiar situations. But it was essential to his argument that this habit-forming process should not merely exist but also be capable of continuous transmission from generation to generation. That this happened and was of primary importance in evolution Butler tried to show by advancing his theory of 'unconscious memory', which was part of each individual's biological inheritance and could be passed on enriched by the new or improved habits formed during the individual's lifetime.

Butler summarized the essentials of his theory in a letter which he wrote to H. J. Nicoll in 1883. He is referring to *Life and Habit*:

> The theory contained in this work turns upon four main propositions. Firstly, that there is a *bona fide* oneness of personality existing between parents and offspring up to the time that the offspring leaves the parent's body. Secondly, that in virtue of this oneness of personality the offspring will remember what has happened to the parents so long as the two were united in one person, subject, of course, to the limitations common to all memory. Thirdly, that the memory so obtained will, like all other memory, lie dormant until the return of the associated ideas. Fourthly, that the structures and instincts which are due to the possession of this memory will, like every other power of manufacture or habit due to memory, come, in the course of time, to be developed and acted upon without self-consciousness. The phenomena of heredity, with its exceptions, such as reversion to a remote ancestor, and

sports ; the principle underlying longevity ; the infecundity of hybrids ; the phenomena of old age ; the resumption of feral characteristics ; the fact that the reproductive system is generally the last thing to be developed, are then connected, and shown to be explicable, and indeed to follow as matters of course, under the joint operation of the four principles contended for.[1]

This theory of evolution, involving the hypothesis of a real continuity of memory between parents and children, embroiled Butler with most of the scientific world of his day. The professional scientists were contemptuous of him, alleging truly that he was not one of themselves and was without any scientific training. He was written down by reviewers, and answered acrimoniously back ; and before long he had a number of quarrels on his hands, including a somewhat undignified wrangle with Darwin himself. The scientists of the day derided Butler's theory, though Darwin in his later editions became more cautious about natural selection as a sufficient explanation of all the phenomena of evolutionary change.

It needs to be borne in mind that Darwinism, when Butler attacked it from the standpoint of a rival theory of evolution, was still relatively new and the subject of very sharp controversy between those who accepted it and those who rejected the entire concept of biological evolution in all its forms. Butler, in upholding the idea of evolution but denying Darwin's version of it, was making sure of the maximum disapproval and playing the lone wolf even more than he had done in *The Fair Haven*. What he was rebelling against was, however, essentially the same thing as was anathema to many Christians—the conception of the living universe, and of man as part of it, as ruled by the blind chance of unexplained biological variations selected by the inexorable laws of a purely material environment. He could make fun of the God of tradition ; but he could not bear to make such fun as this view seemed to make of man.

[1] *Butleriana.* Autobiographical Notes, pp. 11-12.

It was, throughout, of man and of man's place in the world that Butler was thinking ; and he could not endure to think of himself, and of other men, as mere ' sports ', with no real power to shape their own lives. What he was really looking for was a theory, not so much of biological, as of social, evolution, that would allow man a creative role not only as an individual, but as a link in a long chain of succeeding generations participating in a sustained common effort. Part of what he was in search of he might have found, as Durkheim was to find it, in the social transmission of memory through the group, which enabled each generation to pass on its inheritance with additions to the next. But it did not occur to him to give his theory this social shape ; nor would this have solved what was for him the greater part of the problem. He saw Darwin as the destroyer of the foundations of human liberty, as well as of the recognition of any element of purpose in human life ; and he sought to give man back his liberty by insisting that the individual could not only learn by his own effort to master his environment better, but could also transmit this learning through a process of heritable biological adaptation.

The effect of this doctrine was to put the greatest stress on the continuity between parents and children. It involved the fullest recognition of the importance of the family as an agent of social development. This may seem a strange doctrine in one who was at the same time vehemently attacking the Victorian family and demanding the right for the children to live their own lives in defiance of their parents' wishes. There was, however, no inconsistency. Butler regarded the family as the great transmitting agency of acquired habits ; but he also laid emphasis on the need for modifying habits and for growing new ones. The child's business in life was not simply to take over what the parents transmitted, but to build something new on the foundations thus provided ; and Butler saw this as involving an incessant conflict between the parents' wish to keep the child in the old grooves and the child's creative urge to escape—not from his inheritance, but from being limited by it in shaping his own course. It was thus the child's duty to revolt against parental dictation, but not to break right away unless he had to ; for the child needed the conserving as well as the creative forces in order to live well. This, I think, helps to explain why, despite all his abuse and all his quarrelling, Butler never broke right away from his own people.

Butler's books on evolution are not much read nowadays. Indeed, they are so entangled in the controversies of the period following the publication of Darwin's *Origin of Species* as to be none too easy to read. Their influence, however, thanks to Bernard Shaw, has been considerable—not among scientists, who have never taken Butler seriously, but among social thinkers. They have contributed much more to the development of sociological than of biological ideas ; and if modern biologists are less dogmatic about the forces behind evolution than were the Darwinians of Butler's day, the change in their attitude is not to be attributed mainly to his influence. It is, nevertheless, safe to say that his theory of memory looks very much less absurd to present-day scientists than it did to his contemporaries, and that the sociological implications of the argument are much better understood.

Butler wrote the first three of his books on evolution one after another, and while he was doing so wrote little else, except his contributions to *The Examiner* in 1879. Then, with *Unconscious Memory* off his hands, he turned back, with Miss Savage's constant encouragement and help, to re-writing his first draft of *The Way of All Flesh*, at which he worked intermittently from 1880 to 1883, without ever reaching the later chapters. But he also took up with new activities, and during these years his friendship with Henry Festing Jones, whom he had met first in 1876, rapidly ripened. His financial difficulties were relieved in 1880, when his father at length came to terms with him, and he was able to satisfy his urge to travel. But they soon recurred, and in 1884 he was again in serious trouble. For a time, however, he was able to go holidaymaking in Italy, with Jones as his companion, and the outcome was the first of his books about Italian art and people—the delightful and strongly personal *Alps and Sanctuaries of Piedmont and the Canton Ticino*, which Jones and Gogin, the painter-companion of some of his journeys, helped him to illustrate. The book is a very pleasant mixture of holiday-maker's tale and comment, artist's appreciation of the less-known artistic treasures and popular arts of Northern Italy, and Butleriana of a much less acrid sort than he commonly indulged in when he was at home. Butler had been to Italy in his youth ; and, as soon as he was able, he returned there with undimmed enthusiasm. He was not yet at all wealthy—that did not come till his father died in 1886 ; but for a while he felt well enough off to travel pleasantly at no great expense, and to make friends the better because he had to be careful of his money.

Jones's friendship, and his changed financial position, made much difference to his life. Both encouraged him to take up new interests ; and it ceased to matter greatly to him that his books brought him no profit—though of course he grumbled about this none the less in his note-book jottings. In 1883 he seriously took up music, with Jones encouraging him and working at his side. From boyhood, Handel had been, not merely his favourite composer, but his hero, set on a pedestal beside Shakespeare and almost no one else ; and his ambition was to pick up the Handelian tradition and to compose music that would restore it to the world of his own day. After *Alps and Sanctuaries* he published nothing, except a volume of selections from his earlier writings, for four years. Then, in 1885, appeared *Gavottes, Minuets, Fugues, and Other Short Pieces for the Piano*, published under his and Jones's names as co-composers—all unmistakably Handelian, and some of them pleasant, but, alas, without that originality for which he had hoped. More ambitious music followed later : *Narcissus, an*

Oratorio came out, with words as well as music, in 1888, and *Ulysses, a Cantata*—again words and music—was left unfinished at his death, and published by Jones in 1904. In both these works he and Jones collaborated, Butler supplying most of the words and a good part of the music. *Narcissus* had some success in a small circle of friends ; but Butler's music never caught on, or deserved to do so. The British people continued to sing *The Messiah* with gusto, but showed in Butler's lifetime little taste for most of Handel's work. The Handelian revival came later, and Butler had nothing to do with it. He can claim the credit only of the unsuccessful pioneer. In my volume of selections from his works (*The Essential Butler*) I have reprinted a couple of specimens to show what Butler's music was like. The verdict, I fear, has to be ' Not bad '—but no more.

In the same year as the *Gavottes* were published Miss Savage died, and *The Way of All Flesh* was set aside, and never revised further. Her death made a great break in Butler's life, though the ripening of his friendship with Jones had caused her to be less indispensable to him than she had been when he was more alone. Pauli's friendship had been for long past a wraith ; and for many years Miss Savage had been a great way first in his intellectual life. But in the years when he was no longer stay-at-home by compulsion Jones had come to count for more and more, and their music had been a further bond. While he was working away at the Pontifexes he came again closer to Miss Savage ; but he seems to have stopped re-writing *The Way of All Flesh* near the beginning of 1884, and thereafter their correspondence was neither so continuous nor so interesting. It showed signs of flagging well before her death. Towards the last he did not even know of her illness or of the operation under which she died. Butler himself put down this falling-off to his renewed financial worries, which ended the following year with his father's death ; but I think there were other reasons.

At all events, Butler's strongest feeling when Miss Savage

died was remorse. He told himself that he had treated her ill, giving back much too little for what she gave him, and even, when he was feeling under the weather himself, being, in his own word, ' bored ' by her and wishing her anywhere else. He never got over this remorse, which came out again and again in his references to her, both in the edition which he prepared of their letters for publication after his death and in notes which he wrote down from time to time —including one of extraordinary ungenerosity in marked contrast to what he usually said of their friendship.

For more than a year after Miss Savage's death Butler published nothing. Then came the last of his books on evolution, *Luck or Cunning ?* followed in 1888 by *Ex Voto*, the second of his Italian volumes. By this time he was thoroughly well-to-do ; but he continued to live in his bachelor chambers in Clifford's Inn, where he had settled on his return from New Zealand. His luxuries were the engagement of a regular clerk and personal attendant— Alfred Emery Cathie—to whose idiosyncrasies there are many references in the *Note-books*, and regular travel in Italy and Sicily, usually with Jones for companion. As a writer, he had no longer any sense of urgency, and his output was small. In 1886 he stood, unsuccessfully, for the Slade Professorship of Fine Art at Cambridge ; and *Ex Voto*, in which he restored the memory and traced the history of Tabachetti, the artist of the Sacro Monte at Varallo-Sesia, shows that he was deeply engaged in the study and criticism of art. From 1888 to 1890 he also contributed regularly to *The Universal Review*, largely on artistic subjects but also with three long articles on *The Deadlock in Darwinism*, in which he attempted to sum up his quarrel with the Darwinians.

Then, after 1890, he found a new interest—Homer. In 1892 he read at the Working Men's College, and reprinted as a pamphlet, a lecture on *The Humour of Homer*. The following year appeared, first in an article written in Italian and then in an English version, his earliest attempts to prove that Homer's *Odyssey* had been composed in Sicily, and that its scenes could be geographically identified. He wrote further on this subject, in both Italian and English, during the two following years; but his full theory, including his contention that the composer of the poem was a young woman, was launched on the world only in 1897, when *The Authoress of the Odyssey* was published, and as ill-received in the classical world as his books on evolution had been in the world of science. In the meantime he had also been working away at his two-volume *Life and Letters of Dr. Samuel Butler*—his episcopal-headmaster grandfather—to which I have already referred. This appeared in 1896 and, like most of his books, failed to sell. He had put a lot of work into it, largely out of a sense of having done wrong to the memory of a man he had come to admire greatly when he had studied the papers handed over to him on Canon Butler's death. But Butler had no great talent as a biographer, and the Bishop's letters, rather than the grandson's editing, make the book interesting.

Butler had by no means done with Homer when he had launched his theory. In his book he had included a prose summary of the entire poem; and he went on to make a complete translation, first of *The Iliad* (1898), and then, two years later, of *The Odyssey* as well. In both cases he announced his translations as meant particularly for those who were unable to read the original. He translated Homer, not into an artificial 'Butcher-and-Language'[1] filled with poetical diction, but into the plainest modern colloquial prose, treating it as a good story which could be appreciated by ordinary people. Both *The Iliad* and *The Odyssey* had been great popular favourites in their day, when verse had been the natural medium for popular storytelling. But in the modern world, Butler argued, ordinary people expected their stories to be written down in simple prose; and he hoped they would enjoy his versions just as

[1] S. H. Butcher and Andrew Lang published a well-known translation of *The Odyssey* (1879).

he had hoped to popularize neo-Handelian music. Here again, he was before his time. If his translations had been published half a century later as 'Penguins', they might well have had the success which has fallen to Mr. E. V. Rieu's excellent versions.

Between these two translations appeared, in 1899, Butler's edition and interpretation of *Shakespeare's Sonnets*, of which I have said something in the previous chapter. In 1901 he published a new edition of *Erewhon*, with substantial revisions and additions, and followed this up with a sequel, *Erewhon Revisited Twenty Years Later*. This was his last book, published in his lifetime. The end came on 18 June 1902; he had fallen gravely ill in Italy, whence he was brought back, with hope enough to make plans for the future, only to relapse and die. *The Way of All Flesh* was published the following year, and at once acclaimed as a masterpiece. Soon new editions of a number of his books were called for; and his scattered writings began to be collected and reprinted. *Essays in Life, Art and Science*—mainly from *The Universal Review*—appeared in 1904; *Seven Sonnets and A Psalm of Montreal* were privately printed at Cambridge the same year; *God the Known and God the Unknown*—from *The Examiner*—was issued as a volume in 1909. More important were the extracts from Butler's note-books, first published serially in *The New Quarterly* from 1907 to 1910. These were followed by Festing Jones's collection, *The Note-books of Samuel Butler*, published in 1912, and by Jones's two-volume *Memoir* (1919), which contained many further extracts as well as letters and personal recollections. *Butleriana*, including much autobiographical material, followed in 1932, *Further Extracts from the Note-books* in 1934, and the full correspondence with Miss Savage, edited by Butler himself, but with additions from his papers, in 1935. Before this, a collected edition of his *Complete Works* had been published between 1923 and 1926; but this of course did not include the later publications from his papers.

III

EREWHON—AND A SUMMING-UP

While Butler lived, *Erewhon* was by far his best known book. Indeed, no other had reached at all a wide public. Even *Erewhon* was never a ' best-seller ', and brought its author little enough in money. For the rest, Butler paid for the printing and publication of his own books, and usually lost on them. He was incapable of writing anything that he did not really want to write, apart from getting money by it ; and the books he wanted to publish were not such, apart from *Erewhon*, as any large numbers of his contemporaries wanted to read. But with *Erewhon*—and of course posthumously with *The Way of All Flesh*—he did catch the taste of a substantial public. *Erewhon Revisited*, written nearly thirty years later, had no corresponding success, although it is in a number of respects a better book than its predecessor. It has some attempt at characterization—whereas *Erewhon* has none ; it is much more of a story, and much better constructed ; and its satire is not less pointed or effective. To some extent these very merits tell against it. Satire does not go well with delineation of character, especially of characters the author likes. The story does not allow the digressions which make up some of the best of *Erewhon*. The satire is more concentrated on a single theme, and that theme—the growth of the Sun-Child legend—is of a sort to antagonize a good many readers. But the thing that matters most is that *Erewhon Revisited*, as a sequel, could not possibly make its impact with the same freshness and surprise as *Erewhon*. The reader knew what manner of satire to expect, though not the direction in which it would be launched ; and that took some of the gilding off the gingerbread.

In *Erewhon*, from title to subject-matter and from matter to style of writing, Butler first showed his remarkable talent for turning familiar things the wrong way round. Nothing pleased him (or Miss Savage either) better than to invert a proverb or a quotation in such a way as to present a startling thought—a verbal paradox that was much more than a play on words. His *Note-books*, and his correspondence with Miss Savage, are full of such inversions ; and he loved, having made one, to keep on juggling with it for his own— and posthumously for his readers'—delight. In *Erewhon* he juggled in public, but not so much with phrases as with observances and familiar habits which most people had taken for granted. One example is the Erewhonian treatment, not merely of crime as illness, but of illness as crime— a most pleasant conceit, with enough of underlying truth in it to enable the paradox to bear a large burden of elaboration. Another example, no less evocative, is that of the ' Musical Banks ', which proceeds from the paradox of a currency of high moral prestige that lacks all purchasing power to the still more entertaining notion of the Church as a Bank for laying up treasure in heaven by fair pretensions. This is excellent satire on the worldly church-goer, who was much more in the social ascendant then than now. Admirable fun, too, is the goddess Ydgrun (Mrs. Grundy the wrong way round), to whom the Erewhonian ladies gave their real worship. Moreover, *The Book of the Machines* was finely pointed paradox at a time when Darwinism was new, and the controversy between mechanistic and spiritual interpretations of the world raging in every articulate section of society, under the first full impact of science on the popular mind. *Erewhon* was too shocking to become a best-seller, and also too intellectual to be read except by intellectuals. But among intellectuals it was read quite widely, with a sense of novelty and of a number of caps fitted very neatly to the correct heads.

Erewhon had its serious side. Butler meant what he said about the Musical Banks. But for the most part it was a putting out of the tongue at his contemporaries, with no attempt at persuading them. In *Erewhon Revisited*, on the other hand, Butler presented his readers, in the form of a tale, with a development of his theory about the Resurrection, which he had expounded previously in his early pamphlet, and, in a different satirical form, in *The Fair Haven*. The ascent of the Sun-Child into heaven and the subsequent growth of the legend of his divinity are an open and direct satire on the entire supernatural element in the Christian religion, an attempt to show, logically, how the beliefs embodied in it could have developed without any real foundation, and how vested interests could have grown up round them, committed to uphold their influence by all means. This, however well done, could not be quite such fun as the sheer irresponsibility of the paradoxes of the earlier book; and it was bound, being more open, to give even greater offence in many quarters. Last but not least, by the time *Erewhon Revisited* appeared, the Higher Criticism had come to be regarded as *vieux jeu* by many of the intellectuals who were Butler's public. God, and Anti-God, were both rather out of fashion in 1901: indeed, Butler's *Note-books* make it plain that he thought so himself. 'God', he informed an imaginary lexicographer, 'is simply the word that comes next to " go-cart ", and nothing more.'

Nevertheless, Butler could not stop thinking about God, and making notes about him. God had been so dinned into him in childhood, and so closely identified with Canon Butler, that the son could never get either of them out of his mind. Towards both, when he had escaped from them, he achieved a degree of tolerance in retrospect; but essentially he continued to dislike them both, as wielders of irrational and repressive power. This comes out in many passages in the *Note-books*; and *Erewhon Revisited* shows that, even if he had become milder about God, he had not changed his attitude to clergymen or to Churches.

The second main theme developed in *Erewhon Revisited* is largely a repetition of the chapters in *Erewhon* about the 'Colleges of Unreason'. Professors Hanky and Panky and Professor Gargoyle are legitimate successors to Mr. Thims and the Professor of Worldly Wisdom. What is new in the later book is the attempt to paint—say rather, the success in painting—portraits of pleasant people, such as Mrs. Humdrum and the Sun-Child's son by Yram, George.

George, in *Erewhon Revisited*, Towneley, in *The Way of All Flesh*, these are the people Butler most admired, and would most have wished to be like. They are happy, healthy, good-looking, and well-to-do. They understand the world, not from having learnt about it, but by instinct. They have no money troubles, no uncertainties about themselves. They are amiable without cost, because nothing thwarts them. They get what they want without meanness and without trampling upon others. They are kind, because they are kindly by nature; but they do not vex themselves about other people's troubles unless they are obtruded upon them. They do good works when the doing comes their way; but 'good works', done of set moral purpose, they have no use for. Take this, from the *Note-books*, as an epitome. 'To love God is to have good health, good looks, good sense, experience, a kindly nature and a fair balance of cash in hand.' Or this, from the same source: 'Heaven is the work of the best and kindest men and women. Hell is the work of prigs, pedants, and professional truth-tellers. The world is an attempt to make the best of both.'

I know a number of people who do not like Butler's *Note-books*. They find his paradoxical inversions irritating, and many of his preoccupations out of date. It is quite possible to be as allergic to Butlerisms as some people are to puns, and to dismiss his wisecracks as no more than verbal displays. For my part, I enjoy his verbal juggling and the uses he puts it to. I too have lived in Arcadia—or near enough to it to have a lively sense of the absurdities and crampings of that Victorian world. I have encountered, though not in my own upbringing, the Victorian father and his wife: I have come across will-shaking disinheritors, and the shams of pseudo-religious respectability. I have dined, cheek by jowl, with Professors of Unreason : I have met plenty of aggravating dogmatists of science, as well as of religion. These enemies of the spirit of man are fewer than they were, and have to walk more warily ; and now devils a great deal worse have arisen in their place. But, though it would be better to be off with the old devils before we are on with the new, that is not how these things happen. There are enough of the old still left to give Butler's satire continuing point. Its point is, nevertheless, I agree, less penetrating than it was ; and the new devils are well-armoured against it. *The Way of All Flesh*, much more than *Erewhon*, is becoming a period-piece, because the changes in family life have gone further than those in many other fields. The growth of democracy and of the Welfare State has eclipsed the patriarchal father and taxed away the Towneleys' incomes so that they can no longer lord it as they could. 'Three per cents, paid quarterly' are no longer what they were, after two wars and the inflations they have brought with them. 'Good works' have given place to social justice, and 'social workers' have lost their awfulness in the process. It is now possible to be both possessed of a social conscience, and reasonably human and sinful to a moderate degree.

These changes would have perplexed Butler, who was fully as much a child as a critic of his own time. Intellectually, he made daring sallies against his contemporaries ; but he remained tied on a string to many of their conventions. He envied the Towneleys, who could be gentlemen without effort and could carry all before them with hardly a thought ; but he knew that such a way of living was not for him. He was too timid in action, except with a pen ; too much a worrier ; and too self-conscious. He wanted to be respectable, as well as a prodigal : a gentleman, as well as a *gamin*. Above all, once bit by speculation, he wanted to be secure, and at the same time to go his own way, flouting the world's opinion, and yet deferring to it. He sorely needed a confidant who would encourage him to defy the conventions, while observing them; and he found the ideal, in this respect, in Miss Savage. A man thus divided within himself could hardly be generous in giving—not money, but himself. He had always to keep half back, as an inner, secret reserve. That he could be very generous with money his relations with Charles Pauli show; and in that connexion he appears to have squandered his love as well as his money. Perhaps that helped to make him cautious, till, with his future secure and Miss Savage in her grave, he could afford to let himself go when he roved in Italy with Jones for companion.

His achievement as a writer I know not how to sum up. I regard *The Way of All Flesh* as a great novel, despite its falling off in its later chapters—of which Miss Savage was well aware. I regard both *Erewhon* and *Erewhon Revisited* as excellent satires, and the John Pickard Owen memoir in *The Fair Haven* as a little masterpiece in the same *genre*. I believe Butler had something real and important to say about evolution, especially human evolution, though I do not think he said it quite right, largely because he could never disentangle his doctrine of unconscious memory from his quarrel with the Darwinians about Natural Selection. I delight in *Alps and Sanctuaries*, enjoy his Homeric translations, and feel sure he was mainly in the right about Shakespeare's *Sonnets*. I can always quarry happily in the *Notebooks*: I like declaiming *A Psalm of Montreal*; and I am astonished at the excellence of two or three of his few sonnets. But I do not believe that a young woman composed *The Odyssey*, and I doubt if it was composed in Sicily. I am quite unconvinced that either the scientists or the literary critics were in a conspiracy to befoul Butler's name; and I am not prepared to accept his version of his father's character as more than three-parts of the truth, or quite to forgive him some of the ungenerous things he wrote about Miss Savage when his bad mood was on him. In short, I have a strong, but not an uncritical, liking for his books, but, at bottom, no great liking for the man who wrote them.

That, however, from the standpoint of his artistic achievement, is neither here nor there. Butler has what he asked for, and rather more—a narrow, but not precarious, niche in the temple of literary fame.

SAMUEL BUTLER
A
Select Bibliography

(Place of publication London, unless stated otherwise.)

Bibliographies :

A BIBLIOGRAPHY OF THE WRITINGS OF SAMUEL BUTLER AND OF WRITINGS ABOUT HIM. With some Letters from Samuel Butler to the Rev. F. G. Fleay. By A. J. Hoppé (1925).
For additions, notably of later criticism, see bibliography in *Samuel Butler*, par J. B. Fort. Bordeaux (1935).

THE SAMUEL BUTLER COLLECTION AT SAINT JOHN'S COLLEGE, CAMBRIDGE. A Catalogue and a Commentary. By H. Festing Jones and A. T. Bartholomew. Cambridge (1921).
See also Festing Jones's bibliography in *Samuel Butler : A Memoir* (1919) and Bartholomew's ' bio-bibliographical statement ' in Vol. XX of the Shrewsbury Edition of the *Collected Works*.

CATALOGUE OF THE COLLECTION OF SAMUEL BUTLER IN THE CHAPIN LIBRARY, WILLIAMS COLLEGE, WILLIAMSTOWN, Mass. (1945).

Note: The majority of Butler's manuscripts are in the British Museum.

Collected Edition :

THE SHREWSBURY EDITION OF THE WORKS OF SAMUEL BUTLER. Edited by H. Festing Jones and A. T. Bartholomew. 20 vols. (1923–6).
After the death in 1919 of K. A. Streatfeild, his literary executor, Butler's literary estate passed to Festing Jones and after the latter's death in 1928 to A. T. Bartholomew.

Separate Works :

A FIRST YEAR IN CANTERBURY SETTLEMENT (1863). *Travel.*
Reprinted with ' Early Essays ', ed. R. A. Streatfeild, 1914.

THE EVIDENCE FOR THE RESURRECTION OF JESUS CHRIST, AS GIVEN BY THE FOUR EVANGELISTS, CRITICALLY EXAMINED. (Privately printed 1865.) *Theology.*
Issued anonymously.

EREWHON ; or, OVER THE RANGE (1872). *Fiction.*
First edition anonymous. Second edition, revised and corrected (1872) ; new and revised edition (1901). Edited A. Huxley, New York (1934).

THE FAIR HAVEN, by 'the late John Pickard Owen'. Edited by W. B. Owen, with a Memoir of the Author. A Work in Defence of the Miraculous Element in our Lord's Ministry upon Earth, both as against Rationalistic Impugners and certain Orthodox Defenders (1873). *Theology.*
New edition with an Introduction by R. A. Streatfeild (1913).

LIFE AND HABIT : An Essay after a Completer View of Evolution (1878). *Science.*
New edition, with additions and a Preface by R. A. Streatfeild (1910).

A PSALM OF MONTREAL. Leek [1878]. *Verse.*

EVOLUTION, OLD AND NEW : Or, the Theories of Buffon, Dr. Erasmus Darwin and Lamarck, as compared with that of Mr. Charles Darwin (1879). *Science.*
Second edition, with appendix and index (1882). New edition, with author's revisions, appendix and index, edited by R. A. Streatfeild (1911).

UNCONSCIOUS MEMORY : A Comparison between the Theory of Dr. Ewald Hering, Professor of Physiology at the University of Prague, and the 'Philosophy of the Unconscious' of Dr. Edward von Hartmann, with Translations from these Authors and Preliminary Chapters bearing on 'Life and Habit', 'Evolution, Old and New', and Mr. Charles Darwin's edition of Dr. Krause's Erasmus Darwin (1880). *Science.*
New edition, with a Note by R. A. Streatfeild, and an Introduction by Professor M. Hartog (1910).

ALPS AND SANCTUARIES OF PIEDMONT AND THE CANTON TICINO (1882). *Travel and Art Criticism.*
New and enlarged edition, with author's revisions and index, and an Introduction by R. A. Streatfeild (1913).

SELECTIONS FROM PREVIOUS WORKS. With Remarks on Mr. G. G. Romanes' 'Mental Evolution in Animals', and *A Psalm of Montreal* (1884).
Selections from *Erewhon, The Fair Haven, Life and Habit, Evolution, Old and New,* and *Unconscious Memory.*

[LETTERS] to the Rev. F. G. Fleay in *A Bibliography of Samuel Butler*. By A. J. Hoppé (1925).

LETTERS BETWEEN SAMUEL BUTLER AND MISS E. M. A. SAVAGE, 1871–1885. Edited by G. L. Keynes and B. Hill (1935).

Some Critical and Biographical Essays :

SAMUEL BUTLER : A Critical Study. By R. A. Streatfeild (1902).

SAMUEL BUTLER. Records and Memorials. Edited by R. A. Streatfeild. Cambridge (Privately printed, 1903).

DIARY OF A JOURNEY THROUGH NORTH ITALY TO SICILY IN THE SPRING OF 1903 undertaken for the purpose of leaving the MSS. of Three Books by Samuel Butler at Varello-Sesia, Aci-Reale and Trapani. By H. Festing Jones. Cambridge (Privately printed, 1904).

SAMUEL BUTLER, par Jean Blum. Paris [1910].

CHARLES DARWIN AND SAMUEL BUTLER : A Step towards Reconciliation. By H. Festing Jones (1911).

CASTELLIANARIA, and other Sicilian Diversions, by H. Festing Jones (1911).

SAMUEL BUTLER AND HIS NOTE-BOOKS, by J. F. H[arris] (1913).

SAMUEL BUTLER, DER JÜNGERE, 1835–1902. Versuch einer Darstellung seiner Gedankenwelt. Von G. Pestalozzi. Zurich (1914).

SAMUEL BUTLER. A Critical Study. By G. Cannan (1915).

SAMUEL BUTLER, AUTHOR OF *Erewhon*, THE MAN AND HIS WORK, by J. F. Harris (1916).

[SAMUEL BUTLER : AN IMPRESSION] in *Remnants*, by D. MacCarthy (1918).

[RECOLLECTION OF SAMUEL BUTLER] in *Essays, Irish and American*, by J. B. Yeats. Dublin (1918).

SAMUEL BUTLER, AUTHOR OF *Erewhon*, 1835–1902. A Memoir. By H. Festing Jones. 2 vols. (1919).
The standard biography.

GOD THE KNOWN AND GOD THE UNKNOWN. With a Prefatory Note by R. A. Streatfeild (1909). *Theology.*

SAMUEL BUTLER AND *The Press.* Christchurch, N.Z. (1911). *Essay.*
An article extracted from *The Press*, Christchurch, containing reprints of two articles by Butler entitled 'Darwin Among the Machines' and 'Lucubratio ebiria'.

NOTE-BOOKS. Selections arranged and edited by H. Festing Jones (1912).
See also the selection made by A. T. Bartholomew, 1930.

THE HUMOUR OF HOMER and Other Essays. Edited by R. A. Streatfeild, with a Biographical Sketch of the Author by H. Festing Jones, and a Portrait in Photogravure from a Photograph taken in 1889 (1913). *Essays.*
Contains *Essays on Life, Art and Science*, with the addition of *The Humour of Homer*.

[Translation of HESIOD's *Works and Days* (1923)] *Translation.*
First printed by students at the Central School of Arts and Crafts; reprinted in Vol. XIX of the Shrewsbury Edition.

BUTLERIANA. Edited by A. T. Bartholomew (1932).
Mainly unpublished portions of the Note-books, including the curious narrative of Butler's relations with C. P. Pauli, first published in *Life and Letters*, October 1931. A Nonesuch Press edition. Limited to 800 copies.

FURTHER EXTRACTS FROM THE NOTE-BOOKS, chosen and edited by A. T. Bartholomew (1934).

THE ESSENTIAL SAMUEL BUTLER. Selected, and with an Introduction by G. D. H. Cole (1950).

NOTE-BOOKS. Selections edited by G. L. Keynes and B. Hill (1951).
Edited by the literary executors of A. T. Bartholomew.

[LETTER] TO THE ELECTORS OF THE SLADE PROFESSOR OF FINE ART. (Privately printed 1886.)

[LETTERS] to Mr. Edward Clodd in *Memories* by E. Clodd (1901).

[LETTERS] in *Samuel Butler, author of Erewhon: A Memoir.* By H. Festing Jones (1917).

THE LIFE AND LETTERS OF DR. SAMUEL BUTLER, Headmaster of Shrewsbury School, afterwards Bishop of Lichfield, in so far as they illustrate the Scholastic, Religious and Social Life of England, 1790–1840. By his grandson Samuel Butler. 2 vols. (Vol. I January 30th, 1774–March 1st, 1831 ; Vol. II March 7th, 1831–December 4th, 1839) (1896). *Biography.*

THE AUTHORESS OF *The Odyssey*, Where and When She wrote, Who She was, the Use She made of the Iliad, and How the Poem grew under Her Hands (1897). *Scholarship.*
Second edition, corrected and with a Preface by H. Festing Jones (1922). Butler's theory about the authorship of *The Odyssey* had previously been expounded by him in various English and Sicilian papers.

The Iliad OF HOMER RENDERED INTO ENGLISH PROSE FOR THE USE OF THOSE WHO CANNOT READ THE ORIGINAL (1898). *Translation.*
New edition (1914).

SHAKESPEARE'S *Sonnets* RECONSIDERED AND IN PART REARRANGED, with Introductory Chapters, Notes and a Reprint of the Original 1609 Edition (1899). *Criticism.*

The Odyssey RENDERED INTO ENGLISH PROSE FOR THE USE OF THOSE WHO CANNOT READ THE ORIGINAL (1900). *Translation.*
Second edition, with a Preface by H. Festing Jones (1922).

EREWHON REVISITED TWENTY YEARS LATER, Both by the Original Discoverer of the Country, and by his Son (1901). *Fiction.*

THE WAY OF ALL FLESH (1903). *Fiction.*
The posthumous first edition was prepared for the press by R. A. Streatfeild. Reprinted with a Preface by W. L. Phelps (New York, 1916). The Worlds Classics edition (1936) contains an essay by Bernard Shaw.

ESSAYS ON LIFE, ART AND SCIENCE. Edited by R. A. Streatfeild (1904). *Essays.*

SEVEN SONNETS and A PSALM OF MONTREAL. Cambridge (Privately printed 1904). *Verse.*
Edited by R. A. Streatfeild.

ULYSSES, A DRAMATIC ORATORIO in Vocal Score with Accompaniment for the Pianoforte. The Words written and the Music composed by Samuel Butler and Henry Festing Jones (1904). *Music.*

SELECT BIBLIOGRAPHY

GAVOTTES, MINUETS, FUGUES, AND OTHER SHORT PIECES FOR THE PIANO (in collaboration with H. Festing Jones) [1885]. *Music.*
Compositions in the manner of Handel.

HOLBEIN'S *Dance* (1886). *Essay.*

LUCK OR CUNNING, AS THE MAIN MEANS OF ORGANIC MODIFICATION?
An Attempt to throw Additional Light upon the late Mr. Charles Darwin's Theory of Natural Selection (1887). *Science.*
Revised edition (1920).

EX VOTO : An Account of the Sacro Monte or New Jerusalem at Varallo-Sesia. With Some Notice of Tabachetti's Remaining Work at the Sanctuary of Crea (1888). *Art Criticism.*
New edition with additions and corrections (1888). Revised, enlarged, and annotated edition (1889).

NARCISSUS. A Dramatic Cantata in Vocal Score. With a Separate Accompaniment for the Pianoforte. The Words written and the Music composed by Samuel Butler (1888). *Music.*
The Words of the Choruses were privately printed in the previous year. For some account of this curious composition, see *Stepchildren of Music*, by E. Blum (1925), Ch. XVII 'Imitation Handel'.

A LECTURE ON THE HUMOUR OF HOMER delivered at the Working Men's College, London, January 30th, 1892. Reprinted, with Preface and Additional Matter, from *The Eagle* (St. John's College Magazine). Cambridge (1892). *Essay.*

ON THE TRAPANESE ORIGIN OF *The Odyssey*. Cambridge (1893). *Essay.*
Reprinted from *The Eagle*, with a Preface.

A TRANSLATION (attempted in Consequence of a Challenge) (1894). A translation into Homeric verse of a passage from Dickens's *Martin Chuzzlewit*.

SAMPLE PASSAGES from a New Prose Translation of *The Odyssey*. Edinburgh (1894).

SYNOPSIS OF THE LIFE AND LETTERS OF DR. SAMUEL BUTLER, HEAD-MASTER OF SHREWSBURY SCHOOL, etc. By his Grandson. (Privately printed 1894.)

SELECT BIBLIOGRAPHY

SAMUEL BUTLER. Conférence. Par V. Larbaud. Paris (1920).

[THE LIFE OF SAMUEL BUTLER] in *Essays on Books*, by A. Clutton-Brock (1920).
Two essays on Butler.

[SAMUEL BUTLER] in *Aspects and Impressions*, by E. Gosse (1922).

SAMUEL BUTLER, 1835–1902, by C. E. M. Joad (1924).

SAMUEL BUTLER : Critic and Philosopher, by P. J. de Lange. Zutphen (1925).

A HISTORICAL AND CRITICAL REVIEW OF SAMUEL BUTLER'S LITERARY WORKS, by W. G. Bekker. Rotterdam [1925].

SAMUEL BUTLER AND HIS FAMILY RELATIONS, by M. Garnett (Mrs. Robert Singleton) (1926).

[APPRECIATION OF SAMUEL BUTLER] in *Essays on Literature, History, Politics*, by L. Woolf (1927).

AFTER PURITANISM, 1850–1900, by H. Kingsmill (1929).

DIE PHILOSOPHIE DES ORGANISCHEN BEI SAMUEL BUTLER (Mit einer biographischen Ubersicht), Von R. Stoff. Vienna (1929).

SAMUEL BUTLER AND *The Odyssey*, by B. Farrington (1929).

SAMUEL BUTLER DER JÜNGERE. Eine Studies zur Kultur des ausgehenden Viktorianismus. Von K. W. P. Meissner. Leipzig (1931).

SAMUEL BUTLER : A Mid-Victorian Modern, by C. G. Stillman (1932).

SAMUEL BUTLER IN CANTERBURY, NEW ZEALAND, by D. Wilcox. Sydney (1934).

SAMUEL BUTLER : A Chronicle and an Introduction, by R. F. Rattray (1935).

SAMUEL BUTLER, L'ECRIVAIN. Étude d'un Style. Par J. B. Fort. Bordeaux (1935).

SAMUEL BUTLER, 1835–1902. Étude d'un Caractère et d'une Intelligence. Par J. B. Fort. Bordeaux (1935).

THE EARNEST ATHEIST. A Study of Samuel Butler. By M. Muggeridge (1936).

SAMUEL BUTLER ET LE BERGSONISME, par F. Delattre. Avec Deux Lettres inédites d'Henri Bergson. Paris [1936].

SAMUEL BUTLER AND *The Way of All Flesh*, by G. D. H. Cole (1947).

SAMUEL BUTLER, 1835–1902, by P. N. Furbank. Cambridge (1948).

The following books by Samuel Butler are published by Messrs. Jonathan Cape : *The Note-books*, edited by Geoffrey Keynes and Brian Hill, and *The Essential Samuel Butler*, edited by G. D. H. Cole, at 12s. 6d. net ; *The Authoress of the Odyssey* ; *Ex Voto* ; *The Fair Haven* ; *Life and Habit* ; *Shakespeare's Sonnets Reconsidered* ; and *Letters Between Samuel Butler and Miss E. M. A. Savage*, edited by Geoffrey Keynes and Brian Hill at 7s. 6d. net ; *The Way of All Flesh* at 6s. net ; *Erewhon* ; *Erewhon Revisited* ; and *God the Known and God the Unknown* at 5s. net; and *Selections from the Note-books* by A. T. Bartholomew at 4s. 6d. net.

¶ THE Supplements to *British Book News*, which are usually published on the last Monday in each month, may be subscribed for through booksellers on a yearly or half-yearly basis. A year's issues cost £1 post free; six months' cost 11s. post free. Prospectuses are available; and particulars of Supplements already published will be found overleaf. Inquiries should be addressed to booksellers, or in case of difficulty direct to the Publishers, LONGMANS, GREEN & CO., 6 & 7 Clifford Street, London, W.1.

BRITISH BOOK NEWS

A monthly bibliographical journal designed to acquaint the reader with the best British books on all subjects, including those published in the Commonwealth and Empire. It contains bibliographies of specific subjects and articles of general interest to the bookman. Its most important feature is the Book List, compiled by a number of specialists, which occupies the major part of each issue and provides a critical selection of the most important new books and reprints of all kinds, annotated, classified and indexed.

2s. per copy (United Kingdom)

1s. per copy (Overseas)

Annual subscription 10s. (Overseas)

Bound volumes, fully indexed, are available as follows through LONGMANS, GREEN & CO., 6 & 7 Clifford Street, London, W.1 : for 1943 and 1944, 6s. net each ; for 1945, 7s. 6d. net ; for 1946, 12s. 6d. net ; for 1947, 15s. net ; for 1948 and 1949, 15s. net each; 1950, shortly, at 15s. net.

¶ *British Book News* is published for the British Council by the National Book League. Address, BRITISH BOOK NEWS, 65 Davies Street, London, W.1.

Supplements to
BRITISH BOOK NEWS
*

BERNARD SHAW	A. C. Ward
JOSEPH CONRAD	Oliver Warner
G. K. CHESTERTON	Christopher Hollis
THE BRONTË SISTERS	Phyllis Bentley
HENRY JAMES	Michael Swan
JOHN KEATS	Edmund Blunden
E. M. FORSTER	Rex Warner
T. S. ELIOT	M. C. Bradbrook
ARNOLD BENNETT	Frank Swinnerton
BYRON	Herbert Read
WILLIAM BLAKE	Kathleen Raine
BERTRAND RUSSELL	Alan Dorward
TOBIAS SMOLLETT	Laurence Brander
GEORGE ELIOT	Lettice Cooper
OSBERT SITWELL	Roger Fulford
JANE AUSTEN	Sylvia Townsend Warner
G. M. TREVELYAN	J. H. Plumb
SHERIDAN	W. A. Darlington
RUDYARD KIPLING	Bonamy Dobrée
I. COMPTON-BURNETT	Pamela Hansford Johnson
THOMAS HARDY	R. A. Scott-James
SOMERSET MAUGHAM	John Brophy
THOMAS CARLYLE	David Gascoyne
JOHN MASEFIELD	L. A. G. Strong
EDITH SITWELL	John Lehmann
MILTON	E. M. W. Tillyard
R. L. STEVENSON	G. B. Stern
ELIZABETH BOWEN	Jocelyn Brooke
SHELLEY	Stephen Spender

Each with a frontispiece; an introductory essay;
and a select bibliography

PUBLISHED FOR
THE BRITISH COUNCIL
and the NATIONAL BOOK LEAGUE
by LONGMANS, GREEN & CO.
LONDON. NEW YORK. TORONTO.

Revised Price
2s. 6d. net

¶ THE Supplements to *British Book News*, which are usually published on the last Monday in each month, may be subscribed for through booksellers on a yearly or half-yearly basis. A year's issues cost 18s. post free; six months' cost 9s. post free. Prospectuses are available; and particulars of Supplements already published will be found overleaf. Inquiries should be addressed to booksellers, or in case of difficulty direct to the Publishers, LONGMANS, GREEN & CO., 6 & 7 Clifford Street, London, W.1.

BRITISH BOOK NEWS

A monthly bibliographical journal designed to acquaint the reader with the best British books on all subjects, including those published in the Commonwealth and Empire. It contains bibliographies of specific subjects, and articles of general interest to the bookman. Its most important feature is the Book List, compiled by a number of specialists, which occupies the major part of each issue and provides a critical selection of the most important new books and reprints of all kinds, annotated, classified, and indexed.

2s. per copy (United Kingdom)

1s. per copy (Overseas)

Annual subscription 10s. (Overseas)

Bound volumes, fully indexed, are available as follows through LONGMANS, GREEN & CO., 6 & 7 Clifford Street, London, W.1: for 1943 and 1944, 6s. net each; for 1945, 7s. 6d. net; for 1946, 12s. 6d. net; for 1947, 15s. net; for 1948 and 1949, 15s. net each.

¶ *British Book News* is published for the British Council by the National Book League. Address, BRITISH BOOK NEWS, 3 Hanover Street, London, W.1.

Supplements to
BRITISH BOOK NEWS

*

BERNARD SHAW	A. C. Ward
JOSEPH CONRAD	Oliver Warner
G. K. CHESTERTON	Christopher Hollis
THE BRONTË SISTERS	Phyllis Bentley
HENRY JAMES	Michael Swan
JOHN KEATS	Edmund Blunden
E. M. FORSTER	Rex Warner
T. S. ELIOT	M. C. Bradbrook
ARNOLD BENNETT	Frank Swinnerton
BYRON	Herbert Read
WILLIAM BLAKE	Kathleen Raine
BERTRAND RUSSELL	Alan Dorward
TOBIAS SMOLLETT	Laurence Brander
GEORGE ELIOT	Lettice Cooper
OSBERT SITWELL	Roger Fulford
JANE AUSTEN	Sylvia Townsend Warner
G. M. TREVELYAN	J. H. Plumb
RUDYARD KIPLING	Bonamy Dobrée
I. COMPTON-BURNETT	Pamela Hansford Johnson
THOMAS HARDY	R. A. Scott-James
SHERIDAN	W. A. Darlington
SOMERSET MAUGHAM	John Brophy

Each with a frontispiece; an introductory essay;
and a select bibliography

PUBLISHED FOR
THE BRITISH COUNCIL
and the NATIONAL BOOK LEAGUE
by LONGMANS, GREEN & CO.
LONDON. NEW YORK. TORONTO.

Revised Price
2s. 6d. net